The Guid
Owning Tree Boas
and Tree Pythons

Care and Breeding of
Corallus, Sanzinia, and *Python viridis*

CORALLUS CANINUS: PHOTO BY R. D. BARTLETT

Tom Mazorlig

Contents

CORALLUS HORTULANUS: PHOTO BY R. D. BARTLETT

RE-155

© T.F.H. Publications, Inc.

Distributed in the UNITED STATES to the Pet Trade by T.F.H. Publications, Inc., 1 TFH Plaza, Neptune City, NJ 07753; on the Internet at www.tfh.com; in CANADA by Rolf C. Hagen Inc., 3225 Sartelon St., Montreal, Quebec H4R 1E8; Pet Trade by H & L Pet Supplies Inc., 27 Kingston Crescent, Kitchener, Ontario N2B 2T6; in ENGLAND by T.F.H. Publications, PO Box 74, Havant PO9 5TT; in AUSTRALIA AND THE SOUTH PACIFIC by T.F.H. (Australia), Pty. Ltd., Box 149, Brookvale 2100 N.S.W., Australia; in NEW ZEALAND by Brooklands Aquarium Ltd., 5 McGiven Drive, New Plymouth, RD1 New Zealand; in SOUTH AFRICA by Rolf C. Hagen S.A. (PTY.) LTD., P.O. Box 201199, Durban North 4016, South Africa; in JAPAN by T.F.H. Publications, Japan—Jiro Tsuda, 10-12-3 Ohjidai, Sakura, Chiba 285, Japan. Published by T.F.H. Publications, Inc.

MANUFACTURED IN THE
UNITED STATES OF AMERICA
BY T.F.H. PUBLICATIONS, INC.

INTRODUCTION

Snakes rank among the most popular of all reptile pets. Many herp-keepers start with a locally caught garter snake or a captive-bred baby Corn Snake, and, after keeping these successfully, they often want to move on to more challenging and expensive snakes. Perhaps none of the snakes are as surrounded by a reputation for being challenges as are the Emerald Tree Boa, *Corallus caninus*, and the Green Tree Python, *Python [Chondropython] viridis*. These are snakes of nearly unparalleled beauty that are known for being delicate and aggressive. Yet, most advanced hobbyists willing to dedicate sufficient time and money (these are very expensive serpents) to the cause stand a good chance of succeeding with these marvelous animals and several snakes of similar habits, namely the Garden Tree and Annulated Boas, genus *Corallus*, and the Madagascan Tree Boa, *Sanzinia madagascariensis*.

I do not mean that these snakes are for everyone. First, they can be very belligerent snakes. All of these snakes have very large teeth and can inflict nasty, bloody bites. Second, they have very exacting husbandry requirements. Lastly, these snakes can range in price from $150 to well over $2000! Additionally, a few forms are strictly protected, requiring a lot of paperwork to legally import, transport, and own. These are definitely herps for the advanced keeper.

Emerald Tree Boas rank among the most desirable of snakes for advanced hobbyists. Their characteristic deep heat-sensing pits are a rare feature in the true boas, family Boidae, though more common in the pythons, Pythonidae.

W. WÜSTER

TAXONOMY AND REASONING

As you may have already surmised, the snakes covered in this modest volume are not closely related. I have decided to discuss them together because they share similar ecologies, diets, behaviors, and captive needs. With few modifications, the care requirements for one of the species covered will be adequate for any of the others.

Hobbyists sometimes have difficulty telling Emerald Tree Boas *(Corallus caninus)* from Green Tree Pythons. In the boa, the head scales are larger, especially before the eye, and the sensory pits are placed between the lip scales.

While some would classify all of these species in the family Boidae, I recognize Pythonidae as a distinct family. The major reason for this is that all members of Boidae give live birth, but all members of Pythonidae lay eggs, and many exhibit brood behavior. The families show geographic separation as well. Pythonidae is strictly Old World. Boidae is almost strictly New World, but it is also found on Madagascar and the Solomon Islands. There are some skeletal and dentary differences between the two families. To my mind these differences are enough to warrant the distinction between the two groups on the family level. This presents something of a problem when using common names. Boid as used here refers strictly to members of the family Boidae; python to the family Pythonidae. The unusual word booid refers to a member of either family.

Of the species discussed, the

The head scales of the Green Tree Python *(Python viridis)* are uniformly small. Notice the many small scales between the eye and the nostril. The sensory pits are placed within the lip scales, but this can be hard to see. Also notice the brown bars through the eye.

Emerald Tree Boa, *Corallus caninus.*

Emerald Tree Boa, *Corallus caninus,* the Garden Tree Boa, *Corallus hortulanus* [formerly *enydris]*, the Annulated Boa, *Corallus annulatus,* and the Madagascan Tree Boa, *Sanzinia madagascariensis*, are all members of the family Boidae.

There is one other member of the genus *Corallus,* Cropan's Boa, *Corallus cropani* (though it is sometimes placed in the monotypic genus *Xenoboa).* Since this species may be extinct and has never been successfully kept in captivity, Cropan's Boa will not

Garden Tree Boa, *Corallus hortulanus.*

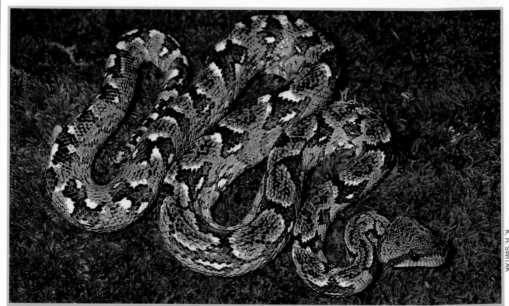

Madagascan Tree Boa, *Sanzinia madagascariensis.*

be discussed any further.

The only member of the family Pythonidae that I will cover is the Green Tree Python, *Python viridis.* Formerly, this species was placed in the monotypic genus *Chondropython*, and later it was included in *Morelia.* Now, many herpetologists believe that *Morelia* is not distinct from *Python* and is, at best, a subgenus. In general, hobbyists have not accepted this

Green Tree Python or Chondro, *Python viridis.*

change, but this is the taxonomy I follow. However, I will often refer to the Green Tree Python as the Chondro or the Chondropython. Readers should also note that when I use the phrase "tree boas" I generally am including *Python viridis*.

ACQUISITION AND SELECTION

Where to Find Them

Because these species are demanding and expensive, most pet stores do not carry them, at least not regularly. If you decide to keep one of these snakes, you most likely will have to find another source. By checking in the classified section of a herp publication like *Reptile Hobbyist,* you should be able to locate several people who are selling the species you want. While most mail-order reptile dealers are scrupulously honest, there are some disadvantages in ordering tree boas and pythons this way. You get no opportunity to make a personal assessment of the animal's health, and you cannot determine how aggressive the individual is. Even careful shipping can be very stressful to snakes, and extremes of weather present unpredictable dangers. Another consideration, especially important with the variable Garden Tree Boa, is that you cannot select the animal for a particular color or pattern. You will have to rely on the dealer's interpretation of your description of the snake you want...not always a good idea.

By far the best way to purchase one of these specialized serpents is to go to a reptile show or directly to a breeder's facility. This will give you an opportunity to examine several prospective purchases and discuss care and breeding at length with the breeder. You can examine the health and quality of the other reptiles as well. This will give you an idea of how conscientious is this particular breeder. An additional advantage to looking for tree boas and pythons at a reptile show is that there are likely to be several breeders present, allowing you to compare prices, housing,

Personally observing a specimen before purchasing it is important. Handling the snake will give you an idea of its health and attitude. Some tree boas and pythons are much more aggressive than others and may be just too much to handle. *Corallus caninus.*

I. FRANCAIS

cleanliness, and other facets of care. Thus, you should be able to pick a healthy individual.

Picking a Good One

Since these snakes are so expensive and relatively delicate, you will want to select one in top condition. An advantage to the high price tag of these snakes is that most will be well cared for. While it is impossible to screen out every possible health problem, there are a few danger signs to watch for. It almost goes without saying that you should avoid buying snakes from dealers who have crowded, dirty, or smelly cages. Do not purchase animals if there are sick or dead animals housed with the others.

One of the most common problems with the tree boas is respiratory infection. Snakes that have encrusted mucus around the nostrils and/or mouth often are suffering from a respiratory illness. Other symptoms include bubbles of mucus in the nostrils, wheezing, and open-mouthed breathing. Snakes showing any of these symptoms are very ill. Do not purchase one as you probably cannot save it.

Poor condition often is readily apparent. This Emerald Tree Boa is obviously dehydrated and sure to have health problems. Notice the accordion-like folds of skin behind the neck and the scraps of unshed skin still on the body. Trouble!

I. FRANCAIS

Corallus cropani, once placed in the genus *Xenoboa*, is restricted to southeastern Brazil. It has not been seen alive in perhaps 40 years and is known from only a handful of specimens in collections. It may actually be extinct.

Another common problem is dysecdysis, a failure to shed normally. The snake will have patches of loose gray skin stuck to its body. Since this usually is caused by low humidity, the snake's skin may appear wrinkled and sunken as well. Low humidity can cause respiratory problems and contribute to visceral gout. Tree boas that are having problems shedding are a risky purchase. Your purchase also sends the dealer the message that the conditions his animals are kept in do not matter; they will sell anyway.

If you can, check the vent to be sure there is no crusted fecal material, a sign of digestive illness. If the jaws look swollen, deformed, or "not right," you should check for mouthrot. Open the snake's mouth carefully (remember these guys pack quite a bite) and look for blood, excessive salivation, and cheesy pus. These are signs of mouthrot and denote a seriously ill animal.

The tree boa you want has firm skin, few wrinkles, no poorly shed skin, eyes not sunken, and no signs of wounds on the body or snout. It should have good weight but not be obese, meaning not having skin showing between the scales or otherwise resembling a stuffed sausage. None of these snakes are known for their docility, so selecting for a mellow one may be fruitless. However, you probably do not want one that strikes furiously each time you walk by the cage.

HOUSING

The housing requirements for these arboreal booids are very similar and so can be discussed together. Later in the text, I will point out modifications that will need to be made for the individual species.

CAGING

The style of cage used for these snakes is critical. They need a tall enclosure. While a glass aquarium in one of the "tall" styles or one turned on its end might work, most keepers opt for other types of caging. They feel that glass aquaria do not allow adequate ventilation, important for these arboreal beauties.

With the increasing popularity of herps has come increased manufacture of products for their specialized needs. With some effort, you may be able to locate vertically oriented cages that allow adequate ventilation. These generally are made from molded plastic, though some have sides of fine nylon mesh (more often used for chameleons; I've heard that some snakes can push their way through the mesh). The ones with sliding glass or transparent plastic fronts are best. This

Adult tree boas and pythons do best in tall, screened enclosures. Though a few suitable commercial cages currently are available, many hobbyists still build their own. Ease of cleaning is essential when planning the terrarium.

I. FRANCAIS

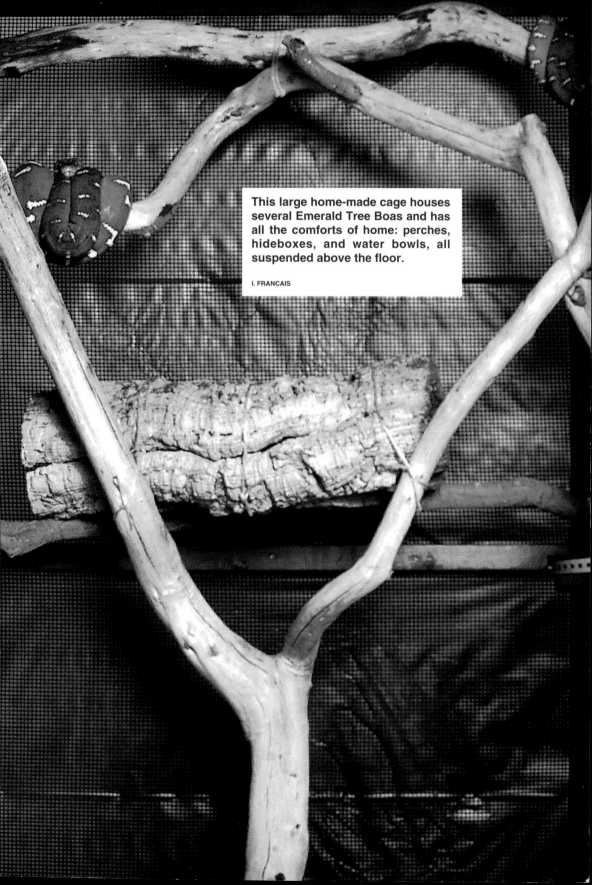

This large home-made cage houses several Emerald Tree Boas and has all the comforts of home: perches, hideboxes, and water bowls, all suspended above the floor.

I. FRANCAIS

provides for easy observation and decreases the chances of escape. Snakes are notorious escape artists, and I'm sure you would not want to find a desiccated green husk in you basement in three months.

Size is also important. None of these snakes are truly giants; most will fall between 3 and 6 feet in length when adult. Keeping in mind the occupant's arboreal habits, a cage should be roughly 2 x 2 x 4 feet, the 4 feet being height. Larger would be better, especially if you plan on housing a pair or a few together. Although many keepers do it, housing more than one of these snakes per enclosure is not recommended.

If you have the tools and knowledge, it may be wise to construct your own cage. Plywood can be used for three sides and the floor. You will want to give these several coatings with polyurethane or another nontoxic waterproofing agent to prevent the cage from rotting in the high humidity. (Be sure to thoroughly air out the cage before use and perhaps also to give it several washings to remove any extra oils or solvents.) The top can be made of plywood or one-eighth inch hardware cloth. If you make the top from plywood, cut a hole in this section and screen it with hardware cloth; this will be where you place the basking light. The front can be made from Plexiglas, hinged to create a door. You will need to incorporate a sturdy locking mechanism into this door design. Hardware cloth may also be an OK choice for a door and

Because of their sedentary nature, smaller tree boas and pythons can be comfortably kept in simple plastic sweater boxes if there is sufficient ventilation.

I. FRANCAIS

Though not especially attractive, newspapers work well as a substrate in a large collection. Newsprint is absorbent, cheap, and safe, and tree boas and pythons seldom come to the ground any way.

would provide for ventilation. If you use Plexiglas for the door, be sure to drill ventilation holes on the other sides and screen them with hardware cloth.

There are many companies and individuals who make customized herp enclosures, including several types suitable for the tree boas. Check the classified ads in a herp magazine or go to a herp show to see what is available. Recently, some pet shops have begun to either stock or special order custom cages, and they also may know someone locally who will make a cage to your specifications, reducing shipping costs. Many keepers find customized shower stalls make excellent enclosures, though they require quite a bit of work to convert.

SUBSTRATE

Different keepers of these serpents use different substrates. As long as the substrate you use is nonabrasive, holds humidity well, resists rot, and is easy to clean, it should work fine. This would exclude gravel, since it does not hold humidity well, can abrade snake skin, and is very unpleasant to clean. Since these snakes tend to eat high off the ground, intestinal impaction from the substrate usually is not a concern.

G. & C. MERKER

Easily available in any pet shop catering to reptiles are many types of wood chip substrates and also pelleted recycled paper products. These may be the most commonly used materials in smaller terraria containing only one or two snakes. Though relatively expensive, they work very well.

Newspaper is probably the most common substrate used by the keepers of these arboreal booids. It is fairly absorbent, inexpensive, and easy to clean. It is not an attractive choice, but it is very practical. Unprinted newspaper may be available locally—check with printers who produce small newspapers such as shoppers and give-aways.

Cypress mulch and packaged reptile bark are good choices as well. They aren't cheap, but they do not have to be replaced often. The feces can be scooped out with a spatula or spoon. Replace all the bark every other month or if mold develops. These beddings hold humidity very well.

Outdoor carpeting and reptile carpeting are used by some keepers. In my experience, these are hard to clean. Unless you want to boil or scrub them for a very long time, stay away from them. Also, they tend not to hold humidity well. This alone would make them unsuitable for use in tree boa cages.

Soft recycled pelleted newspaper makes an adequate bedding. It is very resistant to rot and absorbs several times its weight in water. Like the mulch, feces can be scooped out easily, and it will need replacing only every couple of months. Although I find it pleasant smelling, some people find the scent of this bedding offensive.

Lastly, some keepers keep the bottom bare but covered with about a half an inch of water. This is excellent for providing humidity, but the maintenance is high. The water will need to be changed at least every other day or whenever the snake defecates. The bottom will need to be bleached clean once a week. Standing water may wreak havoc on plywood cage bottoms regardless of paints and coatings. Still, the keepers using this housing method report few problems.

HEATING AND LIGHTING

All of the tree boas are animals of the tropics. As such, they will need heat. Since these snakes are arboreal, it is best to heat them with lights, as opposed to heat rocks, heat tape, or heat pads. These snakes will spend almost no time near the bottom of the cage, so such bottom-type heaters will prove inadequate.

You should suspend a light or two over the branches at the top of the cage. This will create a nice vertical thermal gradient, allowing the snake to move up and down as it wishes to be warmer or cooler. The use of red lights will allow you to heat the cage at night without disturbing the circadian rhythms of your snakes. Ceramic heat emitters will also do this, as they emit heat but no light. If the nighttime temperatures in your house **never** drop below 75°F, heating at night will not be necessary. Realistically, however, almost everyone will have to provide heat at least part of the year.

When setting up the heat lamps, choose a wattage of bulb that will create an adequate gradient. The bottom of the cage

Basking lights and heat emitters will help provide the proper temperature for your tree boas and pythons. Heat emitters help to provide therapeutic, penetrating heat to improve snake health and life-span, without visible light. Photo courtesy of Energy Savers Unlimited.

should be between 75 and 80°F, while the point nearest the lamp should be between 90 and 95°F. The Garden Tree Boa will do well if kept slightly cooler, the hot spot reaching just 90°F. Some field observations suggest that Chondros from the highlands of New Guinea prefer lower temperatures, 85°F being the maximum at which they are comfortable. (You are cautioned that this is an anecdotal report and has not been widely confirmed by keepers and breeders.)

I highly recommend using a digital thermometer with an external probe. The probe can be moved up and down in the cage to get very accurate readings of the temperatures at different places. Most digital thermometers also will store the highest and lowest temperatures in a 24-hour period, allowing you to check for heating malfunctions.

Some keepers recommend the use of full-spectrum lighting in the keeping of these snakes, especially keepers of Chondro Pythons and Emerald Tree Boas. Others seem to get fine keeping and breeding results without it. It seems likely that these snakes would get a fair amount of UV exposure in the wild, so I see no reason not to allow them access to it in captivity. Always make sure there is a shaded area in the cage so the snake can get away from the light if it so desires. Use only full-spectrum bulbs that are manufactured for herps, and replace them according to the manufacturer's recommendations.

The animal must be able to get within one foot of the bulb to receive the beneficial wavelengths of light.

Whether using full-spectrum lights or not, the photoperiod of tree boas should be varied seasonally. This will be almost necessary if you wish to breed them, but it is healthy for the snakes even if you have no plans on reproducing them. In the summer, they should receive about 14 hours of light each day, gradually decreased until they are getting about 10 hours of light each day in the winter. Having your lights on a timer will facilitate this process.

HUMIDITY

For the most part, these arboreal snakes are found in rain forests. This means they are adapted to live in conditions of high humidity. One of the biggest challenges faced by keepers of the tree boas is maintaining adequate humidity. Also, because these are arboreal animals, ventilation must not be sacrificed. Your choice of substrate will affect the ease with which you can keep the humidity high.

When housing tree boas, you should aim for a humidity between 70 and 80%. I strongly suggest buying a digital hygrometer to accurately measure the cage humidity. Combined thermometer/ hygrometer units are available, thus meeting two basic needs with one piece of equipment.

There are several methods you

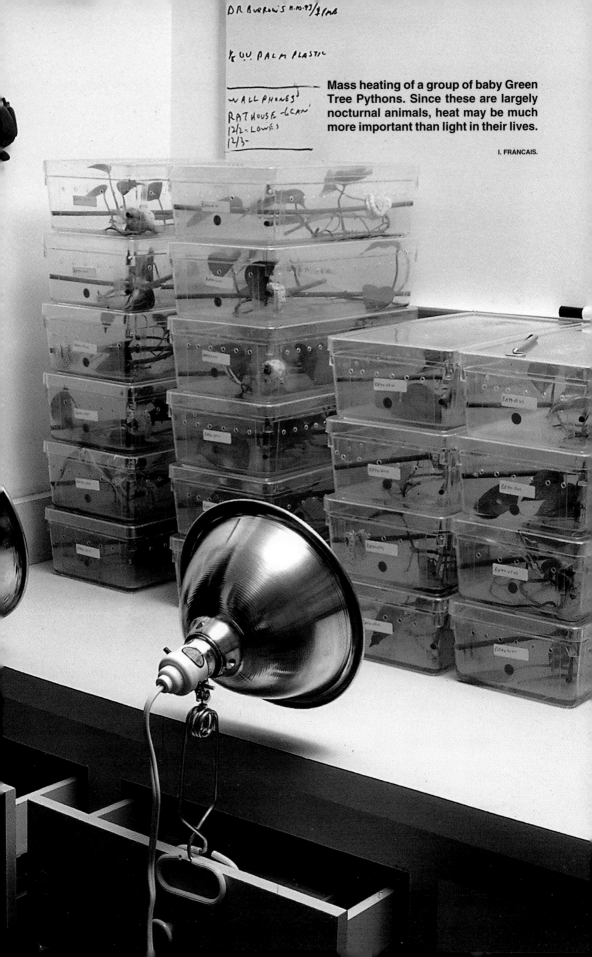

Mass heating of a group of baby Green Tree Pythons. Since these are largely nocturnal animals, heat may be much more important than light in their lives.

I. FRANCAIS.

I. FRANCAIS

Tree boas and pythons tend to have thin skin and dehydrate rapidly. An important part of the daily care is a thorough misting of the cage and also the snakes. The droplets of water that form on the body also may be directed to the mouth of the snake by the scales, making drinking easier.

can use to keep these animals moist. The most familiar method is the plant spraying bottle. This works all right but becomes time consuming in a large collection. Also, the bottles may not be able to provide enough "rain" to elicit breeding. To keep your humidity within the desired range, you probably will need to spray your snake at least twice a day. You also could use a drip system on top of the cage. These are containers that have a spout at the bottom, usually with a valve of some sort to control the flow.

Make sure the water drips over some of the cage furnishings, such as plants or a perch area. Most of the water should end up in a water bowl at the bottom to avoid flooding out the cage; obviously if you have built drains into the cage this is not a concern.

Using a humidifier to keep the whole room humid is a fairly common method. As long as you have adequate ventilation in your herp room, this is an excellent and efficient way to humidify your snakes.

Recently, mini-foggers made for moisture-loving herps have come out on the market. They produce a very fine mist of water (even producing fog effects) that keeps the relative humidity very high. Check your local pet store for information on these.

Though these snakes require high humidity, they also need ventilation. Your terrarium must be designed to ensure that there is sufficient air flow to prevent the rapid growth of molds and other pesky and dangerous plants. A totally sealed enclosure is not necessary or desirable. Finally, remember that basking lights may become very hot and could cause severe burns if the snake were to come into contact with them. Be sure the screen that separates the snake and the lights is sturdy and that there is no gap where the snake could crawl into contact with the light.

HUMIDITY PROBLEMS

If your arboreal booids are not kept humid enough, they will develop health problems. One of the first noticeable signs will be difficulty in shedding their skin. Patches of skin will stick to the snake instead of it all peeling off at once. The brille covering the eye is the most troublesome spot. Keeping the cage humid enough should prevent this. If shedding difficulties occur, mist the snake

Insufficient humidity in the terrarium leads to many problems, one of which is improper shedding of the skin. These baby Green Tree Pythons obviously are not having troubles—note the complete shed skin. Proper perches also are important in promoting healthy sheds.

K. H. SWITAK

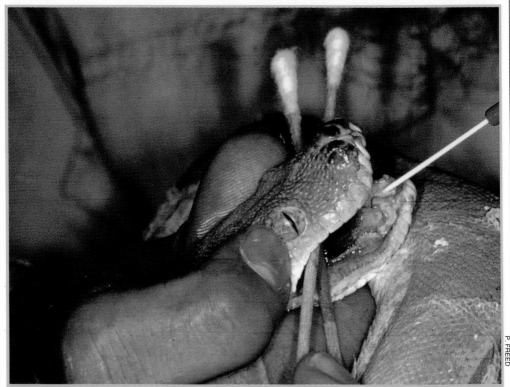

P. FREED

Respiratory infections are common in Green Tree Pythons that are kept too dry. Veterinary care and often a course of drug treatments may save the life of an affected snake, but proper housing certainly is cheaper and less stressful.

heavily and see if the condition improves in 24 to 36 hours.

If this does not work, you will need to make a small humidifying chamber for your snake. Use a container that will hold the snake comfortably but that does not give it a lot of room in which to move. Poke some ventilation holes in the top and/or sides and cover the bottom with sopping wet paper towels. Put the snake in and cover the container. Remember to keep this container some place warm; I recommend keeping it in the snake's cage to help contain an escapee. Check the snake frequently, realizing it will take several hours for the skin to completely loosen.

Respiratory ailments also may develop in tree boas that are not kept humid enough. These are life-threatening if not caught in time, so it is better to prevent them. Neonates are especially susceptible to respiratory diseases, and even experienced breeders occasionally lose a baby or two because of them. Keeping your snake warm, moist, and free of stress is the best way to keep respiratory infections away.

The signs of respiratory infections are myriad: open-mouth breathing, encrustations around the mouth and/or nostrils, bubbly mucus in the mouth and/or nostrils, anorexia, and abnormally frequent or lengthy basking or otherwise staying in the warmest area of the cage. Not all of these symptoms always will be present. If you think your snake has a respiratory ailment, you must take it to a qualified reptile veterinarian as soon as possible. You also should quarantine that animal in a room that has no other herps. Keep the snake under excellent conditions, meaning heating, humidity, etc., must be optimal. You should not allow the temperature to drop at night until the illness is gone completely. You may also want to raise the temperature of the cage five degrees or so. Follow exactly any instructions your veterinarian may give you. I would keep the animal quarantined for at least a month after all symptoms disappear.

OTHER CAGE FIXTURES

For ease of maintenance and observation, the enclosures for these snakes should not be cluttered. It is easier to see, to clean, and to dodge a bite in a relatively empty cage. There are, of course, several items that must be included in the cage if the snakes are to thrive.

A water bowl is a must. This will keep the humidity elevated in between mistings. Most of these snakes will not drink from a water bowl, so some misting is always necessary. There are many observations of tree boas lapping

Give your snake a variety of perches to help prevent stress. Different sizes, shapes, angles, and materials ensure the snake will always find a comfortable resting spot. *Corallus hortulanus* .

P. FREED

water up off their coils, so mist the snakes directly and the cage fixtures, as well. The water in the bowl should be changed at least every other day to prevent a build-up of pathogens. Water bowls must be fairly shallow; some of these snakes have been known to drown in their water bowls. Having some branches, artificial plants, or rocks jutting out of the water will give your snake an exit route should it get into the water bowl and encounter problems.

Perches may be the most important feature of a tree boa enclosure. These snakes may spend all of their time wrapped around a horizontal perch, never coming down to the bottom of the cage. Several perches will be needed at varying heights to allow the snake to thermoregulate. Perches can be made from any number of materials: manzanita branches, wooden dowels, PVC pipes, or natural branches to name a few. The perches should be a minimum of 1.5 inches in diameter; a couple of different sizes will not hurt. Many keepers suggest not using perches that are totally smooth, but others use smooth PVC with no problems. The perches should be removable but fixed enough that they are not able to fall or rotate. Removable perches are very handy for removing the snake while cleaning the cage, and they are also easier to clean. Trying to "unwind" from its perch one of these arboreal snakes is stressful to the snake and potentially painful for the keeper.

It is good to have a hidebox present in the cage. Large bird nesting boxes or even bird houses will work well. They should be suspended well above the floor of the cage, so that the snake does not have to go down to the bottom to use them. I recommend having two shelters, one high up in the cage and one rather low down. This way the snake can pick a comfortable temperature yet remain secure. Having damp moss, soil, and vermiculite in the shelter may help the snake shed as well as turning the shelter into a potential nesting site. Although these snakes may not use the hidebox often, it still is best to include at least one in the enclosure.

There are divided opinions about plants in a tree boa enclosure. While they look nice and help maintain the humidity, they decrease visibility, increase the cleaning chores, and could be harmful to the snake. The harmfulness of plants is based on a record of an Emerald Tree Boa accidentally consuming a plant leaf and dying. (Snakes of course do not eat plants, but they may ingest leaves with the fur or feathers of their prey.) I'm more or less in favor of plants, particularly a nice *Ficus* (ornamental fig) tree whose limbs could serve as perches. If you opt to include plants, they must be sturdy enough to withstand the rigors of a large snake crawling over them, and they must receive adequate light. You may want to keep a few plants as back-ups, exchanging them for any in the cage that start to look too beat-up.

FEEDING

It is in the feeding of tree boas that the superiority of captive-bred stock to wild-caught is quickly revealed. Captive-bred tree boas usually will feed on mice without problems, although the neonates may refuse them. On the other hand, wild-caught individuals may eat only lizards or frogs or refuse to eat entirely. Many of these will need to be force-fed and still are likely to die. The ones that insist on lizards and frogs may never take mice. And, of course, wild-caught tree boas usually have a hefty load of parasites. Save yourself lots of trouble and buy captive-bred tree boas.

A young Emerald Tree Boa feeding on a mouse. Rodents seem to be the main food of all adult arboreal boas and pythons.

K. H. SWITAK

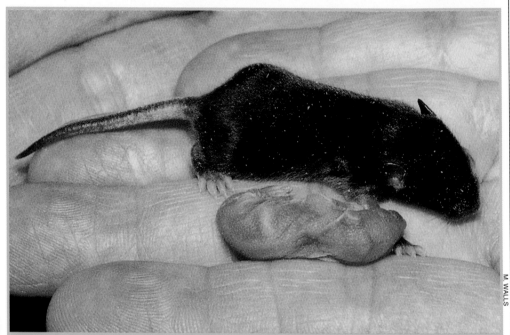

M. WALLS

Mice of all sizes are readily available at many pet shops. Baby tree boas and pythons may need pinkies for a few weeks but then move on to fuzzies or hoppers before accepting adults.

MICE

Mice are probably the easiest and cheapest food to feed your tree boa. They are available at most pet stores that cater to reptiles and are fairly inexpensive. Nearly all captive-bred tree boas will eat mice, at least eventually. Feeding pre-killed mice, either fresh or frozen and thawed, is definitely safer for the snake than feeding live mice: dead mice can't fight back. However, some snakes will refuse any prey that is not alive.

If you have a snake that is reluctant to take pre-killed mice, there are a number of things you can do to coax it into eating them. I first would try simply warming up a pre-killed mouse. Often this will induce the snake to eat the dead mouse, especially if the

mouse was frozen. Wiggling the mouse with forceps can help as well (don't use fingers or you may get bitten), and you can progress to lightly tapping the snake on the face with it. Once the snake is angry enough to strike, it usually will hold on and swallow. After the snake grips the mouse, let go gently and make no sudden motions; you don't want to scare it into dropping the food.

If the tree boa you have eats live mice and you want to feed it pre-killed ones, you can try scenting a pre-killed mouse with a live mouse. To do this you just rub the dead mouse with the live one. Be careful not to get bitten by the live mouse. If your snake is not eating mice at all, try scenting a pre-killed mouse with a lizard. You can rub a mouse with a

The labial pits of Green Tree Pythons (here a red juvenile) allow them to detect the body heat of living mammal prey. Some arboreal boas and pythons will refuse non-living prey, but most adapt if you are patient.

K. H. SWITAK

whole lizard or, if this fails, dab the mouse in a mixture of puréed lizard and water (disinfect your blender afterwards!). Frogs work nearly as well with young snakes, and you should definitely try them if scenting with a lizard fails. One of these scents should be attractive to your booid. After a few of these scented meals, the snake will usually eat unscented pre-killed mice without problems.

If none of these methods work, try feeding your snake in a small, darkened enclosure. Only do this with pre-killed or pinkie (newborn, hairless) mice; older live mice may turn on the snake, causing horrible wounds and possibly death. You can also try small lizards and frogs that cannot harm the snake. I've had good results using this feeding method with a wide variety of snake species. After only one or two meals, most snakes will start to eat in their regular cages.

Neonatal (newborn or newly hatched) snakes generally can go some time without food, as there is some yolk still stored in their gut. Many will not take a first meal until after their first shed, often at least a week after coming into the world. However, you must be careful not to let the animal starve. If the spine or ribs are plainly visible, the baby snake is dangerously emaciated. You should intervene well before this point, force-feeding or having a veterinarian force-feed the serpent for you. Do not try to force-feed your snake until a veterinarian or experienced person shows you how. You easily can injure or even

kill a snake by improperly force-feeding it. Force-feeding is an art best learned by tutoring and then careful practice.

I cannot say how long the baby snake can go without eating, as there is much individual variation. A rule of thumb would be that even if the snake seems in good condition, if it hasn't eaten in six weeks you should seek veterinary care. Remember that most individuals will not eat until after they shed for the first time, which can take up to 14 days after hatching or birth. Also, if temperature and humidity are not in the preferred ranges, a snake may not eat, nor will the snake eat if it feels insecure. Make sure the snake has enough cover and a hidebox.

Most pet stores carry mice and rats, live and often frozen. If your local pet store does not stock rodents for feeding, there are quite a few companies that will ship rodents to you. Several of these companies carry chicks as well. Normally there is a minimum order of 100 mice or so, and shipping may be expensive.

Raising mice and rats is not difficult, but it is time- and space-consuming and in the long run probably doesn't save a lot of money, as you need cages, bedding, food, etc. Always raise rodents in a different room from the snakes. The constant odor of the rodents can cause snakes to stop eating and to be aggressive. You must always wash your hands after handling the rodents, because if you smell like a rodent you must be a rodent (at least

Mice and rats fed to boas and pythons must be treated humanely and fed on an excellent diet themselves. Cheap rodents from undetermined sources may be deficient in essential nutrients and vitamins.

from the snake's point of view). Many snake bites occur because keepers fail to wash their hands after handling feeder rodents. Please be kind to the mice you raise; they may be food, but they have a right to humane treatment.

Mice or rats that are fed a balanced diet can form the whole diet of a tree boa. The balanced diet is important; a rodent fed a poor diet makes a poor meal. You should inquire as to what your pet store or mouse supplier is feeding to their rodents. Since the snake eats the whole animal, if the animal is well-nourished the snake receives a nutritionally

Some hobbyists believe that pinkie mice are deficient in calcium and thus must be supplemented by dipping their rumps in calcium powder. Their mother's milk, however, is an excellent calcium source, and other hobbyists believe supplementation is unnecessary.

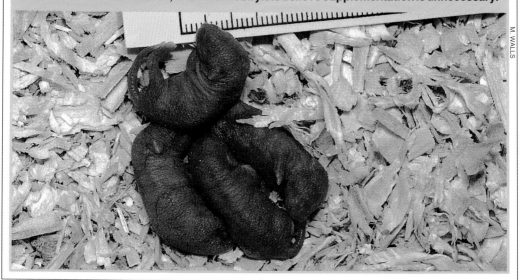

complete meal. Nearly all of the mouse is digested, including the skeleton, a rich source of minerals. Snakes that are eating whole mice probably don't need any supplemental vitamins.

The mice you feed to your tree boa should be no bigger around than the snake is at midbody. Using this guideline, you should never have a problem with the snake having to regurgitate prey that is too large (messy, smelly, and stressful to the snake).

Young tree boas need baby mice, called pinkies or fuzzies depending on whether or not they are old enough to have hair. Since the skeletons of baby mice are not fully formed, many herpeto-culturists believe that they do not contain enough minerals, specifically calcium. If your snake is eating primarily pinkies and fuzzies, it may be wise to use a calcium supplement every third feeding. To do this wet the rump of the mouse and dip it in the calcium powder. Some keepers disagree with this, saying that the milk in the mouse's digestive tract is rich in calcium. I tend to supplement pinkies occasionally. You will have to make up you own mind when it comes to supplements.

OTHER FOODS

In addition to mice, most tree boas will take lizards, birds, and, sometimes, frogs. Neonates often insist on frogs or lizards for their first few meals. Small Cuban Treefrogs (*Osteopilus septentrionalis*) often work well, as do small anoles. Both of these

Green Treefrogs, *Hyla cinerea*, are available over much of the year and can be obtained through any good pet shop. Hatchling and newborn tree boas and pythons may insist on small frogs or lizards for their first few meals before moving on to rodents.

K. H. SWITAK

M WALLS

Many people think baby chicks are just too cute to use as snake food, but individual tree boas and pythons may express a preference for birds as food. If desperate, you also can try small finches from a pet shop.

animals frequently are available at pet stores. Green Treefrogs (*Hyla cinerea*), a widely available North American species, also might entice your snake to eat. Small gecko species may be available cheaply and can be tried. After a few meals of lizards and/or frogs, most neonates will begin to take mice without a problem. Some keepers feed tree boas rat pups instead of mice. These are a little larger, and some snakes seem to prefer them to mice. A number of keepers feed chicks to their snakes, sometimes exclusively and sometimes in addition to mice and rats. A diet high in birds tends to make your snake produce loose and odoriferous feces but otherwise creates no problems.

Although it has often been repeated that the tree boas have developed their enlarged teeth to penetrate the feathers of birds, the stomach contents of these snakes only rarely include birds. The enlarged teeth probably have developed simply to ensure that the prey is securely held in the mouth. Tree boas and pythons often are ambush predators, lying quietly in wait for a rodent that comes close enough for one strike. That one bite must securely grab the prey, because dropping prey out of the top of a tree would be a waste of food and energy. Based on the stomach contents, mammals make up the majority of the diet of adult tree boas. Lizards and frogs also frequently are eaten. Interestingly, insects are occasionally found in the stomachs of young *Corallus*. It is not clear if the snakes ate the insects or if they came from the stomachs of ingested lizards and frogs.

M. SMITH

Are laboratory rodents just too fat to be fed to snakes? Some keepers think so and try to culture wild rodents instead. Wild mice and rats often prefer a seed diet that produces less fat under the skin.

PROBLEMS

The tree boas as a whole are not active snakes. Frequently, those kept in captivity are overfed and become obese. You should prevent this, as an obese snake can suffer from many of the same problems that plague obese humans. Additionally, obese snakes often fail to breed. To prevent obesity, you should feed adult snakes only once every ten days to two weeks. Neonates and juveniles can be fed more often, but you must watch for signs of obesity.

A few breeders have begun to wonder if laboratory mice simply are too fatty to provide a satisfactory regular diet for tropical snakes. They suggest breeding and feeding leaner types of mice, such as captive-bred deer mice and white-footed mice. At the moment, such "diet" foods are not widely available. Most keepers have never had problems with carefully feeding laboratory mice to their snakes.

During breeding, and occasionally for no discernible reason, tree boas will stop eating. These periods of inappetence may last days to months. As long as your snake appears healthy, there is no need to worry. Keep offering food and eventually your snake will start to eat again. If this fast lasts longer than three months or the snake starts to look emaciated, you should take it to a vet.

TREE BOAS: EMERALD, GARDEN, AND ANNULATED

The genus *Corallus*, widespread throughout tropical America, contains both the most common and the rarest of the snakes in this book. The Garden Tree Boa (*C. hortulanus*) is a readily available and relatively affordable snake available as wild-caught and captive-bred animals. The Annulated Tree Boa (*C. annulatus*), on the other hand, is a rather rare snake in captivity, and few exist even in academic collections and zoos. Somewhere in between is the Emerald Tree Boa (*C. caninus*), a prized serpent that now is being bred in fairly good numbers by both hobbyists and commercial breeders.

Corallus as a genus is easily distinguished from most other snake genera; only *Sanzinia* and *Python viridis* could be confused with it. As with the other arboreal booids, *Corallus* has the head well distinguished from the neck and has deep, obvious pits on both the upper and lower labials (lip scales). However, unlike similar genera, in *Corallus* the scales on top of the head are erratic in placement but large, and the loreal scales (between the eye and nostril) are few in number. Small

Though the Emerald Tree Boa, *Corallus caninus*, may be the most photogenic species of the genus, it has no real advantages over the other species except color. Emeralds fortunately now are being captive-bred in decent numbers.

R. HUNZIKER

R. D. BARTLETT

Red phase *Corallus annulatus* are attractive animals, but they really are not typical of the appearance of most Annulated Tree Boas.

scales are interposed between the loreals and the supralabials (upper lip scales), and these small scales continue under the eye. There is no visible frontal scale. This genus is rather infamous for the large and recurved anterior teeth, which most individuals are happy to show off. In cross-section the body is oval to triangular. The tail is long and strongly prehensile. The scales are smooth, never keeled. Like the other boas (family Boidae in the strict sense), these snakes give live birth.

ANNULATED TREE BOAS

As I have stated, the Annulated, or Ringed, Tree Boa is the least frequently kept and bred of the tree boas. Indeed, most hobbyists will never see this snake at all. Little is known of its natural history, and it actually may not be that rare in the wild, but it seldom is seen or collected. Distinguishing this snake from the Garden Tree Boa relies mainly on scale counts, although most Garden Tree Boas are more attractively colored and patterned.

Description

The background colors of *C. annulatus* are rather dull, ranging from brown to gray. The belly is a dingy yellow to beige. Reddish ovals bordered by gray adorn the sides. These markings usually are more or less obscure but can be very distinct. There are 40 to 45 of these ovals, and they often meet over the back. Brown specks and spots may be numerous over the head and belly. Neonates are bright red to nearly black and attain adult coloration in one or two years. These boas average roughly 3.5 feet in length when adult, with a record near 7 feet.

Although the Garden Tree Boa has a proportionately longer tail than the Annulated, scale counts are the only sure way to tell these two boas apart. *C. annulatus* has

76 to 86 subcaudals (scales under the tail), while *C. hortulanus* has 100 to 130. Because *C. hortulanus* shows very variable and intricate colors and patterns, general appearance is not always a reliable way to distinguish the two species. The Annulated Tree Boa has 50 to 55 rows of dorsal scales at midbody and 252 to 273 ventral scales (scales down the belly from under the head to the vent).

sparse in scientific collections, three subspecies have been described, two from South America. The two South American subspecies are based on small differences in rostral scalation and appear doubtful. However, there are some good scalation differences between South American and Central American individuals. It has also been suggested that the Annulated Tree Boa is a composite built of a few

A nice, fairly typical Annulated Tree Boa. This species is hard to distinguish from the much more common Garden Tree Boa without checking scale counts. The longer tail of the Garden is especially obvious.

Natural History

This boa has been little-studied since its description by Cope in 1876 (as *Xiphosoma annulatum*). Its range is Nicaragua south to Ecuador; it now has been found in tiny populations in Honduras and Guatemala as well. Although

similar species. Because of the limited data, I hesitate to recognize any subspecies at all.

The life history and ecology of the Annulated Tree Boa are poorly known. The only thing positively known about its habits are that it is secretive and arboreal. It is thought to hunt on the ground at night, presumably for mammals, lizards, and birds. This boa has been found in open and rather overgrown areas and occasionally can be found in banana plantations. Scientists think that Annulated Boas mate in the dry season, giving birth in August through October.

Breeding

The Annulated Tree Boa is not frequently bred by zoos, and I know of no hobbyists who have bred this animal. Mating occurs during a slight cooling from December to February, and the young are born from July to November. The females will bask heavily throughout gestation and may continue eating as well. Basking ceases just before giving birth. Eight to thirteen young are present in a litter. Colors in one litter can run the gamut from orange to red and brown through black. Many will not eat on their own until a few months old. Some, however, will voluntarily feed on frogs, pinkies, hatchling quail, and lizards. These boas reach sexual maturity around four years of age.

EMERALD TREE BOAS

A true living gem, the Emerald Tree Boa evokes all the beauty and mystery of the rain forests in which they dwell. They have a reputation for being aggressive and difficult to keep, yet they are

Most Annulated Tree Boas found for sale are wild-caught adults that may carry scars and parasites. Few successful breedings of this species have been recorded, and the snake appears to be uncommon to rare even in nature.

W. WUSTER

R. D. BARTLETT

A typically marked Emerald Tree Boa, *Corallus caninus*, "a beautiful challenge." Though captive-bred, this beautiful snake remains expensive to purchase and seldom is an easy snake to maintain.

eagerly sought after and command a high price. Perhaps they can best be described as a beautiful challenge.

Description

As their name suggests, Emerald Tree Boas are bright green when adult. Generally, the ventral surface is yellow. The green sides and back may be solid, but more frequently there are white markings. These are generally in the form of small diamonds or triangles running down the spine, sometimes fusing into a scalloped stripe, but there is a lot of variation. Some individuals have largish white spots low on the sides that may be outlined with black or blackish green. The young are born reddish or orange to yellow with bright white bands across the back. They change to green a few scales at a time over the first two years of life. Often the head changes color after the rest of the body.

Adult Emerald Tree Boas easily can be distinguished from all other arboreal booids, save one, the Chondropython. Chondros and Emerald Tree Boas are remarkably similar to each other, despite being only distantly related. The similarities extend to the neonatal colors, the adult colors, the curious flatly coiled perching position, and other details of their arboreal lifestyles. Many hobbyists confuse them, and it can be hard to tell the species apart in photographs. The major easily seen differences between them involve the head scalation and the shape of the snout. The heads of Chondros are covered in fine scales all the way differences in the labial pits in pythons and boas, but they are hard to see unless you have a cooperative specimen. The difference is that boas have their labial pits *between* the labial scales, while pythons have each pit *within* a labial scale. Without actually handling the snake, you may not be able to see this

R. D. BARTLETT

This Emerald Tree Boa displays the obviously enlarged scales covering the top of the snout that mark the species. Not all specimens have such large scales, however, so you also have to check for large loreal scales (in front of the eye) if you worry about confusing the species with the Green Tree Python.

down to the nasals, so there are just two large scales on top of the head. The heads of Emerald Tree Boas have fine scales that are replaced on top of the snout by much larger scales. The nasal scales of Chondros are large, which gives the snout a very bulbous look compared to that of the Emerald Tree Boa. There are difference. It is better to rely on the head scales. Also, most breeders wouldn't lie about which animal they're selling, so you can trust them when making inquiries.

While adult Emerald Tree Boas are easy to tell from the other members of *Corallus*, the young can be hard to distinguish from

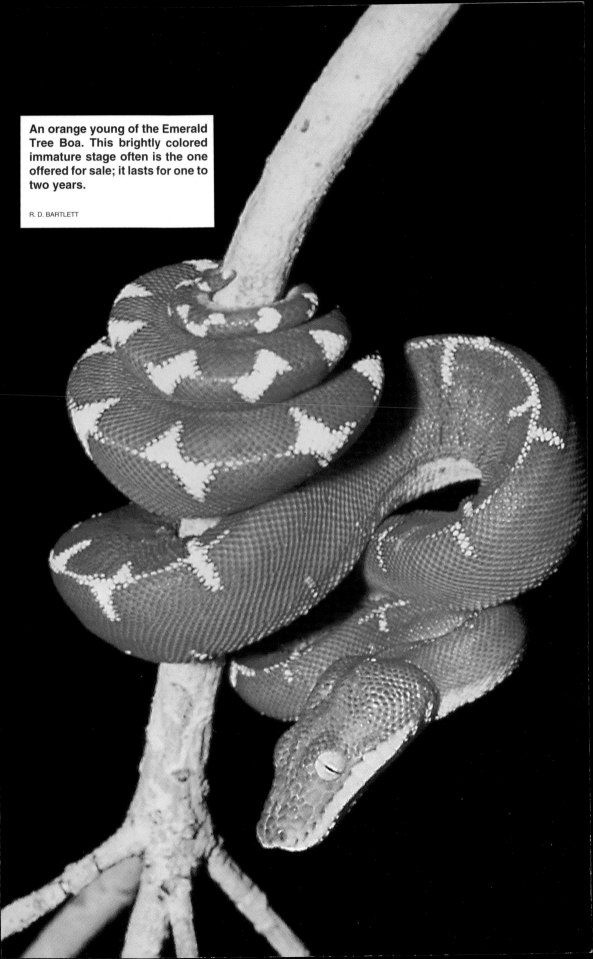

An orange young of the Emerald Tree Boa. This brightly colored immature stage often is the one offered for sale; it lasts for one to two years.

R. D. BARTLETT

those of the other species. Emerald Tree Boas have shorter tails than Garden Tree Boas and, consequently, have fewer subcaudal scales, only 64 to 79. Emeralds have 188 to 219 ventrals, and their dorsal scales are in 61 to 74 rows at midbody. These are the largest of the arboreal booids, averaging 6 feet, with a record of nearly 10.5 feet.

Natural History

C. caninus exists over quite a large range covering much of northern and central South America. It occurs in rain forests of the Amazon basin and additionally is found in forests of drainage systems in Colombia, Ecuador, Surinam, and the Guianas. It

Adult Emerald Tree Boas are longer than most other arboreal boas and pythons, often exceeding 6 feet in length. They still are graceful animals, however, with a relatively slender shape and well-proportioned body.

MARIAN BACON

can be found as far south as northern Bolivia. In this wide range, the snake usually is not common.

The young boas are not as strongly arboreal as the adults, staying within a few yards of the ground. As they turn green, they move into the treetops. Like the Chondropython, Emeralds will spend most of the day resting in a flat, symmetrical coil on a horizontal branch. Their coloration provides excellent camouflage as they perch high amongst the leaves. At night Emeralds may hunt actively, even venturing down to the forest floor. However, they also will grab meals that come too close to their resting perch. They prey mainly on mammals; birds and lizards are taken as well, especially by juveniles. Emeralds breed in the spring, as the dry season turns into the rainy season.

Although some keepers and breeders distinguish between Emeralds coming from the Amazon basin and those coming from the Guyanan Shield (the northeastern part of the snake's range), few descriptions of differences exist in the scientific literature. Breeders generally claim that the Amazonian Emeralds have a much better temperament than the Guyanan snakes. They also say there are differences in head scalation and

The typical resting pose of the Emerald Tree Boa is unusual, the body coiling off the perch in regular U-shaped loops, the head lying square in the middle of the loops. Curiously, the distantly related Green Tree Python also has this resting position.

that the Amazonian boas have a complete or nearly complete white dorsal stripe. Usually the Amazonian boas command much higher prices than Guyanan. I'm not sure the two names describe anything more than local variations within the species, but further research may prove the distinctions to be valid.

Husbandry

These snakes can be housed as described earlier, but since Emeralds are a little larger than the other snakes a larger cage may be in order. The humidity must remain above 70%. Dehydrated Emeralds will darken in color until they are nearly black (and, consequently, nearly dead).

Breeding

Breeding Emerald Tree Boas in captivity is not the rarity it once was. However, they are still challenging to breed, and perhaps beyond the capabilities of the average hobbyist. Breeding these snakes requires patience, time, and a careful attention to details.

Probing is probably the best method to sex Emeralds (and other tree boas). Note, however, that females can sometimes probe rather deeply, to six or seven subcaudals, though two or three subcaudals is more typical. Males probe very deeply, usually to 14 subcaudals. Males generally have larger spurs and a thicker tail base than females, but probing is by far the most accurate way to sex these snakes.

In their equatorial natural range, Emeralds experience only slight differences in temperatures over the year, and seasonal variation in temperature is mild. So, for the Emeralds, only a small temperature drop is needed to stimulate mating and reproduction. At night the temperature during the cooling period should be 66 to 69°F, while

Probing successfully determines the sex of almost all Emerald Tree Boas. Males have much deeper hemipene pockets than females.

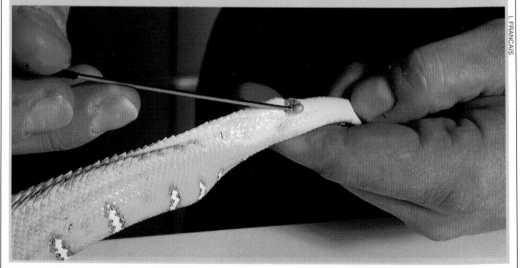

I. FRANCAIS

the daytime high temperature should be reduced to 80 to 82°F. During this cooler period, the humidity should be lower as well; let the humidity drop to about 70%, no higher. This reduced temperature and humidity period should last roughly two to three months. After this period, gradually increase the temperature and humidity to normal keeping levels.

You will have better success in breeding Emeralds (and most of the other snakes in this book) if you can arrange for simulated showers in the enclosure. When you start increasing the temperature, set up your raining or misting system so that it precipitates in the boa's cage for 10 to 15 minutes in the morning and 10 to 15 minutes in late afternoon or early evening. You should keep this routine up for two to three weeks and then return to normal keeping conditions. If you have no provisions for simulated rain, mist the snakes **heavily** in the morning and evening, trying to get the humidity to about 95%. It is critical that the ventilation in the enclosure be optimal during your "rainy season," or mold will grow like mad.

Most breeders advocate keeping the sexes separate outside of breeding attempts. It is well documented that separation of the sexes is one the most, if not the most, critical components in the breeding of Emeralds and many other booid snakes. Four to six weeks into the cooling period, introduce the female to the male's cage. Mating often will not occur until the wee hours of the morning. Usually they mate on their perches, but sometimes they will use a hidebox. Remove the female in 24 hours and reintroduce her to the male every few days throughout the rest of the cooling period. The reason for the reintroductions is to allow the pair to mate multiple times, which leads to higher levels of fertility. Never house more than one male in an enclosure, especially during the breeding season. Vicious fights will ensue, and severe injuries or even death may result.

Females will give birth five to seven months after mating. It is important that the female have access to an adequate range of temperatures during gestation. Gravid females will spend prolonged periods of time basking, keeping their body temperature high. They generally will stop feeding within two months of mating, but some eat throughout gestation. Feeding smaller than normal meals may enable the female to keep eating longer during gestation, which is probably healthy for her and the neonates. Most females will move to a cool area of the cage shortly before giving birth.

The young are clad in colors ranging from brick-red to orange-red, rarely yellow or greenish, at birth. They will set about climbing almost immediately. Normally, 7 to 12 boas are born in a litter, but the range is roughly 2 to 20, each about 16 inches long. Mothers that went off their food will resume eating within a day or two after parturition.

Young Emeralds are delicate. Greatest success in rearing them occurs if they are housed individually and kept very humid. Many breeders advocate using 2.5- to 5-gallon fish tanks with a quarter inch of water covering the bottom. Others use moistened paper towels and include a sizable water bowl. If a water bowl is used, be sure to rig up a way for the neonates to get out, such as a rock that comes above the surface or a piece of artificial plant that leads out of the bowl. Cage fixtures for the babies should be like those of the adults but on a miniature scale. Temperatures

Because they dehydrate readily and sometimes succumb to respiratory infections, young Emeralds can be considered delicate snakes and thus not suitable for the beginner or any keeper who does not have time to supply all their needs.

P. FREED

Garden Tree Boas, now *Corallus hortulanus* but until recently called *C. enydris*, are extremely variable in color but usually have a pair of dark stripes behind the eye. This plus their very long tails will distinguish them from the other arboreal boas.

should be kept in the middle of the temperature range as neonates are not nearly as temperature-hardy as the adults. Enticing baby Emeralds to feed can be difficult, but the strategies outlined in the feeding chapter should work. Remember that these are difficult snakes, and even seasoned breeders will occasionally lose a few neonates. If you suffer a few losses, console yourself by thinking that breeding Emerald Tree Boas at all is quite an accomplishment.

GARDEN TREE BOAS

The Garden Tree Boa appears to be the most common of the snakes in this volume. Although frequently bred, it is just as frequently wild-caught, the imports being stressed, irascible, and difficult charges. Like so many other reptiles, imported Garden Tree Boas usually do not survive. Wild-caught individuals may be cheap, and captive-bred neonates range in price to about $200, depending on the color and pattern of the specimen. Recently, the Garden Tree Boa's scientific name was changed from *Corallus enydris* to *Corallus hortulanus*, or I should say changed back, as this was the name by which it was known until roughly 1935.

Description

The Garden Tree Boa is a complex species that is one of the most variable of all snakes. Aside from great pattern and color variation between individuals, there is variation over the life of an individual, and there may be little relation between the colors at birth and the colors at adulthood. Two subspecies have been described, but many herpetoculturists, myself included, believe the variability in

K. H. SWITAK

Recently *C. hortulanus* was broken into several species that may be distinguished by small and often externally invisible characters, so they are of importance mostly if you plan on breeding your snakes. To be on the safe side, always try to breed specimens from the same or at least close localities. Almost all of South America (except the northwest) is occupied by typical *C. hortulanus* (top), while Central America to Trinidad would be the home of *C. ruschenburgeri* (bottom).

P. FREED

this taxon is too great and too understudied to fit into definable subspecies.

The traditionally recognized subspecies are *C. h. hortulanus* and *C. h. cooki*, the latter often called the Cook's Tree Boa. The two are separated on the basis of range and scale counts. Cook's Tree Boa is found throughout Central America into Colombia and Venezuela and also on some Caribbean islands. The range of the nominate form covers the majority of South America, south as far as Bolivia. *C. h. cooki* has under 50 rows of dorsal scales at midbody, while *C. h. hortulanus* always has 50 or more. There is a tendency for *C. h. hortulanus* to have more ventral scales, usually 270 to 299; *C. h. cooki* generally has 253 to 275. These are not strong distinctions, and there is no gap in the counts. Color patterns cannot be used to reliably separate the subspecies.

It long had been suggested that there are more than one species hiding under the name *Corallus hortulanus*, and a recent (1997) revision of the species by Henderson actually broke the species into four separate species. Two of Henderson's species are restricted to the southern Caribbean: *Corallus grenadensis* on the Grenada Bank and *C. cooki* (used in a different sense than traditionally accepted) restricted to St. Vincent. Specimens from Central America and northwestern South America (to the Orinoco basin and Trinidad and Tobago) are called *C. ruschenburgeri*, while those from

R. D. BARTLETT

Also seen on occasion, especially in zoos, is the Garden Tree Boa from Grenada in the Lesser Antilles. If distinguished, it would be called *C. grenadensis*.

the rest of South America are *C. hortulanus* proper. The distinctions among these species are very narrow and difficult to judge, and it is not certain that most herpetologists will accept these changes. Fortunately, virtually all wild-collected specimens belong to the typical South American form, and so do most captive-bred specimens.

Garden Tree Boas have the general *Corallus* features including a wide head on a skinny neck, oval cross-section, and long recurved teeth. They have the typical ornery disposition as well; in fact, this may be the snappiest of the snakes covered in this book. No small scales separate the nasals, and the internasals are large. The eyes are ringed with

12 to 17 scales that separate them from the supralabials. There is one huge preocular and two oval loreals, also rather large. The pits are deep except for the ones between the anterior infralabials, which are rather weak. Both subspecies have 100 to 130 subcaudals. Adults of this species may be up to 9 feet long, but generally they are closer to 3.5 feet. Garden Tree Boas stay very slender for their length.

Color in this species is so variable as to nearly defy description. Adult coloration usually is a washed-out yellowish or grayish brown. Down the back runs a line of small oval spots of a darker shade, alternating with smaller diamonds lower on the sides. The spots commonly have pale centers. Individual scales may be outlined in brown, often producing brownish circles. The ventral scales may range from dingy yellow to almost white, often lightly to heavily marked with dark blotches. Bright red crops up in the patterns of some snakes, often with the dorsal spots outlined in red or yellow. Some can be uniformly red, brown, or yellow animals, while others may be nearly black with dark spots outlined in yellow (this form sometimes is called the "garden phase").

Most Garden Tree Boas have heavy markings on their heads in

Corallus hortulanus is the most adaptable tree boa and has the widest range (assuming it is just one species) of the genus *Corallus*. It also is relatively unspecialized and can tolerate drier conditions than the other species, including areas that man has modified. Garden Tree Boas are much closer to being beginner snakes than are Emerald Tree Boas.

R D BARTLETT

Just some of the variations found in Garden Tree Boas. Many different colors and patterns may appear in a single litter. Though there are hints that some differences may be genetic in origin, pure-bred color forms have yet to be produced.

V. T. JIROUSEK

the form of dark stripes running from the eye to the corner of the mouth, often outlined in white that separates the stripe from another on top of the eye that runs to the back of the head. The lips usually are marked with dark spots or lines. Any and all colors and patterns can be found in one litter.

Natural History

Although not often seen in nature, Garden Tree Boas are widespread and common snakes. They rest high in the trees during the day, becoming active after sunset. These are very adaptable snakes, being found in both humid and relatively dry situations in many types of forest and even in savanna environments. As a general rule, they prefer less humid conditions than Emeralds. They can be found close to human habitations, including gardens, plantations, and the edges of villages. Rarely are these snakes encountered on the ground; they hunt mammals, lizards, and frogs up in the trees. Some data suggest that young specimens may take insects. This may be the most active species of this group, ranging far and wide across interwoven tree branches to hunt. Generally this species breeds in the spring, as temperatures and humidity start to rise, but as a species they can breed throughout the year.

Because Garden Tree Boas are so variable in color and pattern, the keeper should look at many specimens to find one that suits their personal tastes.

R. D. BARTLETT

Husbandry

These snakes can be housed like the other tree boas, though humidity is not as crucial to the well-being of this animal as it is to most of the others. Temperatures in the range of 80 to 90°F are adequate. Garden Trees are a little more active than the other tree boas and therefore would enjoy a slightly larger cage. Young and wild-caught specimens are especially bad about taking rodents, and it may take considerable time and effort to convert them from the lizards, frogs, and birds they may prefer.

Breeding

Often Garden Tree Boas will breed without any conditioning on the part of the keeper. Mating takes place from January to June, with young being born from May to November. Most breeders do, however, condition their snakes. There are some indications that changes in the photoperiod are an especially important reproductive clue in this species. The photoperiod should gradually be shortened to 10 hours of light in mid-winter and gradually lengthened to 14 hours in mid-summer. Keep them slightly drier and cooler in the winter as well for the best chances of success. In the spring, begin spraying the snakes heavily. Separation of the sexes appears to be unnecessary most of the time, but if you do keep males and females separate, place the female in the male's cage about a week after raising the temperature and humidity. Allow your pair to copulate several times by housing them together for several days. Once you believe the female to be gravid, she should be kept separately.

Early in gestation, gravid females will feed heavily and bask often. Feeding her small meals will allow her to feed longer during gestation. In general, females will stop feeding around a month before giving birth, but this varies greatly, with some eating until a week before parturition. Gestation will last six to seven months. Garden Trees normally give birth late at night. Many color patterns can be present in one litter, some of which may seem to bear no relation to the patterns of either parent. Litters range from 4 to 20 young that measure around 14 inches.

Young Garden Tree Boas should be housed individually to avoid cannibalism and to give you a better idea of whom is eating what. I recommend marking on each enclosure what the inhabitant is eating. The neonates will shed in two to three weeks after birth and then will be ready to be fed. Try pinkies, but have other foods ready in the likelihood that some of the neonates are stubborn. Once feeding readily, they usually are hardy. Sexual maturity is reached in four or five years.

Despite attractive colors and the interesting variation, Garden Tree Boas are not very popular. This may be due to having all the disadvantages of Emeralds and Chondros but little of their beauty.

MADAGASCAN TREE BOAS

Sanzinia madagascariensis, the Madagascan Tree Boa, is one of the hardest to find of the snakes covered in this book, probably second only to the Annulated Boa in rarity. And, of course, *Sanzinia* has a price that matches its scarcity. I've seen it at reptile shows priced at $1,500! This certainly is not the snake for everyone.

DESCRIPTION

Sanzinia madagascariensis (the only species of the genus) has a fairly triangular head that, like other arboreal booids, is strongly set off from the neck. There are deep vertical pits set between the labial scales on the upper and lower jaws. This is a distinctly stocky snake with a short,

prehensile tail. A vertical pupil is set in the small eye.

The scales on the head are small and granular instead of being formed into more normal shields. Raised tubercular scales often are found on the head as well. Occasionally specimens have obvious prefrontals, and the internasals are perceivable on most individuals. Up to three supralabials enter the eye. The subcaudals are single and number between 30 and 50. At midbody there are 40 to 50 rows of scales, and the ventrals number between 200 and 235.

Like the Chondro and the Emerald Tree Boa, the Madagascan Tree Boa undergoes a large change of coloration with age. The young boas are brownish

The granular to almost tubercular scales on top of the head are fairly typical of Madagascan Tree Boas and help separate them from the Madagascan land boas and South American *Corallus.*

K. H. SWITAK

to reddish brown, turning to shades of green, olive, and olive-brown in about a year. One variation on this theme occurs in some individuals from northwestern Madagascar, where these snakes tend to be born brown and stay that way.

In the normally colored adults, black or greenish black triangles on the sides contrast with the dull greens of the rest of the body.

Internally, the musculature of *Sanzinia* is distinct from related snakes, sharing similarities with the Madagascan (ground) boas in the genus *Acrantophis*. It also shares a chromosome number with this genus that is different from other boids: *Sanzinia* and *Acrantophis* have 17 pairs, while *Boa* has 18 pairs and *Corallus* 20 or 22 pairs. Although *Sanzinia* and *Acrantophis* share several features,

Like some other tree boas and pythons, the young of *Sanzinia* may be quite different in color from the adults. Most young run toward red or reddish brown, becoming more olive or greener with age and sometimes eventually turning dull brown.

R. D. BARTLETT

These triangles frequently fuse in the middle of the back, producing vague hourglass shapes. The hourglasses can be completely or brokenly outlined in white. Normally there is no pattern on the head other than a dark line running from the eye back along the angle of the jaws. The belly of an adult Madagascan Tree Boa normally is yellow. Like the other tree boas, *Sanzinia* is not one of the giant snakes. Adults commonly are 3.5 to 5.3 feet, up to almost 9 feet.

they are different in hemipenis structure, labial pitting (*Acrantophis* lacks pits), and behavior. Though some workers recently have synonymized *Sanzinia* with *Boa* or *Acrantophis*, it appears divergent enough to warrant its own genus.

NATURAL HISTORY

As far as known, it appears that most *Sanzinia* in the hobby are from eastern coastal Madagascar, a humid lowland area. These boas give birth to reddish young that turn greenish on maturity. As noted, those originating in northwestern Madagascar are born rather brownish and do not change color. Northwestern Madagascar is a dry, semi-arid area, and it is possible the *Sanzinia* from this area are a separate species or subspecies from the other *Sanzinia*. Few individuals from the northwestern population are in captivity.

This boid is the least arboreal in behavior of the species discussed. Indeed, *Sanzinia* is often found on the forest floor, especially at night. Presumably, like *Python viridis*, *Sanzinia* hunts on the ground at night. Adults eat small mammals, while the young probably focus on lizards and frogs. These boas often are active at dawn and dusk, as well as in full darkness. There are indications that *Sanzinia* becomes torpid and inactive during Madagascar's dry season,

running from June to August. They generally breed after this, as the Southern Hemisphere spring brings more moisture.

Sanzinia is found occasionally in and around human habitations, adapting well to the edges of villages and cultivated areas. This arboreal boid can tolerate a wide range of humidity levels, which contributes to its success in environmentally disturbed areas. Travelers to Madagascar claim these serpents are abundant along forest edges and widespread across the eastern and northwestern parts of the island. Despite its current abundance, development on Madagascar is proceeding rapidly and potentially threatens this taxon. Currently it is listed as Appendix I on CITES (thus an endangered species requiring loads of permits for legal exportation and virtually no commercial sales), but captive-

Though a few scientists have combined the Madagascan boas (including *Sanzinia*) with the American boa constrictors, genus *Boa*, the deep vertical pits between the lip scales of *Sanzinia madagascariensis* easily distinguish it from *Boa*.

R. D. BARTLETT

bred specimens (assumedly from legal imports before increasing restrictions) are widely available though expensive. If you buy a *Sanzinia*, make sure it has the correct legal documentation to prevent possible problems later.

and exportation of *Sanzinia*, captive-breeding efforts are necessary to supply the hobby. Even given moderate breeding success, this species is likely to always remain a rarity within the hobby. It is delicate, hard to

Old Madagascan Tree Boas become very chunky snakes and often lose much of their distinct greenish coloration. Gravid females become especially dark and muddy in color.

HUSBANDRY

The housing of *Sanzinia* is typical for the tree boas, and it will do fine under the general housing conditions described earlier. As mentioned, the humidity is not that critical a factor for this boa, and levels as low as 50% can be tolerated occasionally; a level near 70% is probably better for long-term care. Temperatures should range from 82 to 90°F during the day and settle to 72 to 75°F at night.

BREEDING

Because of the heavy restrictions on the importation

breed, and present only in small numbers. If breeding does become more frequent, problems related to inbreeding are likely to occur given the small gene pool currently available.

Given these obstacles, keepers of *Sanzinia* still do occasionally breed their snakes. Sexing *Sanzinia* often can be done by looking at the cloacal spurs. Males have much larger spurs than females. If there is any doubt, probing will resolve it. Males will probe to a depth of 8 to 10 subcaudal scales, females only to 2 or 3. To initiate breeding, the sexes should be separated and cooled for roughly two months.

Temperatures should drop to about 84°F during the day and 67 to 70°F at night. Lower the temperatures gradually, over a week or so, and bring them back up in the same fashion. After they have been brought back up to the active temperature and started feeding, introduce the female to the male. Reintroduce the female several times over the next few days. Once the introduction provokes no more copulations, you should leave the female in her own cage to gestate the young.

As with some other boas and pythons, male-male combat may stimulate mating in reluctant animals. Some studies seem to indicate that allowing males to fight over a female results in higher levels of fertility. However, this can be a dangerous process for both snakes and keeper. Bring together the two males and the female in one cage. Watch **closely**. Combat in *Sanzinia* proceeds rapidly, and once dominance of one male over the other has been established, quickly remove the losing male. The pair usually will copulate right after the subordinate male is gone.

When removing the loser, be careful to avoid being bitten; remember you will be dealing with two seriously upset boas. You should remove the subordinate male before any serious damage occurs. Dominant male boas and pythons have caused fatal injuries to subordinate males. Treat any gashes the loser receives with an antiseptic and keep an eye on them. Wounds that are serious or that become infected will need veterinary attention immediately. Because of the danger to the animals, use this method only if absolutely necessary.

One of the first indications you may have that your female is gravid is a darkening of her colors. This change will begin at the first shed after mating. She may become darker, almost a black-green, as the gestation period continues, or darken during that first shed and not change further. The reason for this change in coloration is not known, but most workers assume that it allows the female to absorb more heat from the sun. To my knowledge, no other booid snake exhibits this phenomenon.

In roughly six months, the female will give birth to up to a dozen young, occasionally as many as 16. Most will escape from the birth sac quickly, but be prepared to help those that do not, carefully snipping a hole in the birth sac with surgical or cuticle scissors. The young will measure 16 to 19 inches.

House the young individually, as cannibalism has occurred with this species. Keep them fairly humid, roughly 80%, and otherwise house as an adult. One to two weeks after birth, the young will molt for the first time and then should begin feeding. *Sanzinia* has a reputation for having a strong preference for lizards during the first months of life. Breeding *Sanzinia* is still very sporadic, and there is much left to learn about all aspects of its life.

CHONDROS,
OR GREEN TREE PYTHONS

It is fortunate that Chondropythons are not aware of the changes their taxonomy has undergone in the past decade or so. If they were, the poor snakes could very well be suffering from identity crises. Chondros were recognized in 1875 by Meyer as *Chondropython azureus* (based on a preserved specimen that had turned blue), though the species *viridis* was described a few years earlier by Schlegel. This generic name remained unchanged until it was merged into *Morelia* by Wells and Wellington in 1984. Many workers no longer recognize *Morelia*,

K. H. SWITAK

Chondros (shortened from the old generic name *Chondropython*) are bright green when adult and have the head and snout (including the area in front of the eye) covered with very small, uniform scales. The scales around the nostrils typically are enlarged and even bulbous, however.

synonymizing it with *Python* (see Walls, 1998, *The Living Pythons*, T.F.H.). Thus, the Green Tree Python has gone from *Chondropython viridis*, to *Morelia viridis*, to *Python viridis*. Confused? For the hobbyist,

however, the Green Tree Python will probably always remain the Chondro.

DESCRIPTION

With the notable exception of the Emerald Tree Boa, Chondros are unlikely to be mistaken for any other snake. The two snakes share the same deep green coloration and often are marked with white down the spine. With some careful attention to details, the two species can be distinguished reliably: head scalation and the arrangement of labial pits will separate the two serpents. Unfortunately, these characters can be hard to see in photographs or without getting very close to the snake's head (potentially dangerous with this group of snappy snakes). Chondros often have an enlarged, squarish snout due to the bulbous nasal scales.

They also have uniformly fine scales covering their head, including the top of the snout, while Emeralds will have more regular, larger shields in front of the eyes on top of the snout. In Chondros, the labial pits are situated within the labial scales, rather than between them, as in Emeralds. In Emeralds the pits are found over almost the entire length of the upper lip (certainly to under the eye), while in Chondros the pits in the upper lip scales are restricted to the front of the jaw. Both of these snakes share the odd perching position that is so often seen in photos, a relatively flat coil with the head located in the center. The young of both species are colored in reds, browns, and yellow, changing to green upon maturity.

As in most of the other arboreal booids, Chondros have numerous enlarged labial pits. Because of their great size, these pits tend to distort the contours of the face. The back of the head is rather bulbous. There is a pair of enlarged scales around the nostrils, usually a pair of somewhat enlarged internasals behind or between the nasals, and there are as many as 60 loreals, but rarely are any other head scales distinctly enlarged and comparable to the nine normal head scutes of typical snakes. Two supralabials enter the eye, which otherwise is surrounded by 11 to 20 small scales. There are a total of 12 to 16 supralabials and 14 to 18 infralabials. The posterior infralabials become rather square shaped, while the anterior ones are vertically oriented rectangles. Unlike most other pythons, the mental groove (under the chin) of Chondros is bordered by granular scales rather than more normal-sized ones.

Although you will hardly need scale counts to confirm the identity of a Chondro, I provide them for the sake of completeness. At the midbody, there are 55 to 57 rows of dorsal scales. Ventrals number 219 to 254. There are 68 to 130 pairs of subcaudals, and a few to many of these can be undivided. In length, these snakes average 4 to 6 feet, with a maximum size near 8 feet.

As has been noted, Chondropythons are colored very similarly to Emerald Tree Boas, being clad mostly in deep, emerald green. Some of these snakes tend toward bluish in their coloration and sometimes turn bluish with age. This is especially true of older females, although they generally will retain some green on their heads. There are also individuals that are a purer, deeper blue; whether a blue color is caused by genetic or environmental factors is uncertain. The belly of normal green specimens is bright yellow, with yellow lips as well. The bellies and lips of blue individuals are white or very pale yellow. Some normally colored Chondros will have white lips as well.

Scattered over the body, but concentrated along the spine, are tiny white spots. These are sometimes fused into blotches,

Green Tree Pythons vary greatly in color even at birth. These year-old specimens, all from the same litter, show just how variable they can be until full maturity, when the bright green color scheme appears.

and some individuals have a nearly complete, irregular stripe down the back due to the fusion of the spots. In a few individuals, small yellow blotches will be present, evidently areas of the body that did not turn green upon reaching maturity. The end of the tail usually is not green, instead being nearly black. Baby Chondros have bright yellow tail tips. Like baby Emerald Tree Boas, hatchling Chondros are red, brown, or yellow, normally turning green gradually over the first year of life.

NATURAL HISTORY

Most of the Chondros in the hobby originated from the lowland rain forests of New Guinea. The species also occurs on some of the small islands to the west and south (notably the Aru islands) as well as in northeastern Queensland, Australia. They can be found in a variety of forest types throughout this area, ranging from open to dense, rainforest to drier habits. However, typically these are rainforest snakes. They can be found in the highland areas of New Guinea, not being limited to lower altitudes. Throughout most of this area, there is a pronounced wet and dry season. It is much cooler and drier during the dry season, while during the wet season it can be near 100% humidity and near 90°F most of the day.

During the day, Chondros are inactive, resting coiled around a nearly horizontal branch and relying on their camouflaging colors to keep them safe. When night falls, they travel down

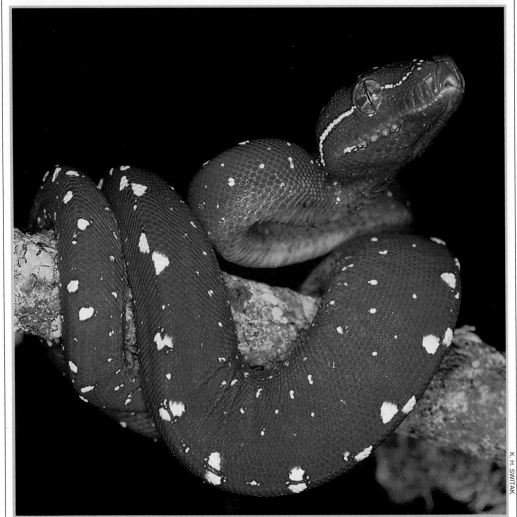

K. H. SWITAK

A brilliant rusty red juvenile Chondro. Displays of captive-bred Chondros may be among the most colorful for any snake. Remember that these colors are not permanent, however.

their tree and hunt on the ground. The majority of the prey of adult tree pythons are mammals, but some lizards are eaten as well. The juveniles tend to feed much more heavily on lizards than the adults. In nature, this helps decrease the competition for food by members of the same species. I can find no documented evidence that this species eats birds, though this is commonly said of the species. Given their nocturnal, terrestrial hunting habits, it would seem unlikely that they would encounter many birds.

The brightly colored tail-tip of the juvenile serves an important function. There are reliable reports of young pythons twitching their tail like a worm to lure lizards within striking range. There are even reports of adults using this behavior to obtain food.

Successfully housing Green Tree Pythons requires a tall, very humid terrarium that never becomes stagnant. This 18-month-old pair gives a good idea of the large head, heavy body, and bright colors of adults.

HUSBANDRY

There are no major differences between housing Chondros and housing the other arboreal booids. Tall, humid, ventilated cages are a must. The basking site should reach 90-95°F, and the humidity should be kept above 70%, up to 100% during a shed. There is some field evidence that Chondros originating in the mountainous regions of New Guinea may do best at cooler temperatures, especially at night.

BREEDING

Chondros probably are the most frequently bred species in this volume. This speaks more of their popularity than it does of the ease of their captive production. Make no mistake, Chondros are quite a challenge to breed and even more of a challenge to rear. However, like most of the other snakes discussed, it certainly is possible for the dedicated and informed hobbyist to breed Green Tree Pythons.

As with most snakes, the most accurate method for sexing Green Tree Pythons is probing. Males will probe to nine or ten scales and the females to only two or three. Spurs are present and are larger on the males, but this is not a truly reliable method. Like other booids, female Chondros grow longer and heavier than males.

Chondropythons may breed and lay eggs nearly any time of the year. Indeed, this python is one of the most aseasonal breeders in the group, both in the wild and in captivity. As long as the keeping conditions are optimal, there is always a chance your Chondros could breed. Additionally, many breeders have noticed that

Chondros most often copulate right before rainstorms, which is unfortunately not a controllable condition. However, if you know a major storm is coming, it would hardly hurt to move the female in with the male.

The best method of ensuring your Chondros breed is to cycle them, with the sexes housed separately. Temperatures gradually should be dropped to about 73°F, with a slightly warmer basking spot. Photoperiod should be reduced to 9 to 10 hours a day and the humidity brought down to about 70%. Remember to give your Chondros about two weeks of fasting before you start cooling them so that they can digest any food that is in their guts. After six to eight weeks, you can start gradually returning the conditions to normal.

Breeding Chondros will be more likely to occur if you have a rain system of some kind. You should initiate your artificial rainy season when the temperatures in the cage are approaching the normal keeping level. Turn on the rain for ten minutes or so in the morning and for a like period in the evening. If you cannot set up a rain system, due to expense or cage design, you will have to mist your pythons **heavily** and **frequently**. You want simulated showers and a humidity level near 100%. Introduce the female into the male's cage once you start to raise the humidity. Leave the pair together for a week or two, as multiple matings will result in increased fertility.

Chondropython males are notorious for fighting viciously with each other. They should never be housed together. Females may be housed together in large cages without problems, and males and females also may be housed together. In some circumstances, reluctant Chondros may be induced to breed by allowing the males to fight in the presence of the female. This procedure can be very dangerous for the snakes; be prepared to intervene should things get too ugly (very likely).

Female Chondropythons usually go off their food when gravid. Like the Emerald Tree Boas, you may be able to keep your female Chondropython eating for more of her gestation period by feeding her small meals. This probably has beneficial effects on the female's health. Gestation lasts from 60 to 90 days, with 70 to 78 days being average.

Unlike all the other snakes in this volume, Chondros lay eggs. Therefore, the keeper must provide in some way for incubation of the eggs. Like other pythons, female Chondros will coil around their eggs and incubate them themselves. Many keepers feel this is the best way to incubate Chondros, while many others feel that artificial incubation is the best method. In this case, the jury is still out, as excellent hatching rates can be obtained by either method.

Before incubating your Chondro eggs, you must provide a spot for the female to lay them. Females

At nine months of age, this male Chondro already is becoming green. In only two years he will be looking for females and may engage in serious fighting with any other adult males in the terrarium.

K. H. SWITAK

not given a suitable nesting site will lay them in the water bowl or drop them from their perch. Either situation is a disaster, as the eggs will drown or burst. For a nest box, you can use any sort of container that has a removable lid and a snake-sized hole in one of the sides. Bird nesting boxes and modified plastic food storage containers are commonly used. Remember that the box has to be large enough to hold a pyramid of eggs with the female python coiled around them. You should place several nest boxes at various heights in the cage, allowing the female a choice of conditions. Line the bottom of the nest boxes with some **barely** damp sphagnum moss. In most cases, the female will choose a box and contentedly lay her eggs. Clutches average 18 eggs, but frequently more or fewer will be laid. The record size clutch is 26 eggs.

Now, if you want to leave the eggs with the female, there is little else to do except wait until the eggs hatch. To allow the mother to successfully incubate her eggs, the cage humidity must be kept at 90 to 100 per cent, and the temperature should not drop below 78°F. The moss in the nest box should never get more than just barely damp. If the moss is too wet, the female may develop blisters or other skin ailments. While incubating their eggs, female pythons occasionally push one out of the pile and off to the side. Remarkably, these eggs are almost always infertile. It is presumed that these eggs smell different from the fertile ones to the mother.

If you wish to incubate the eggs artificially, you should have an incubator set up and the temperature inside it calibrated to 88 to 90°F. The incubator should also have a humidity level of roughly 90%. Most keepers use vermiculite as the incubation medium, mixed 1:1 by weight with water. Air circulation is critical to successful Chondro egg incubation. Your incubator should have multiple air holes (which may compromise the stable environment you need to create), or you must open the incubator every other day or so. The failure to provide fresh air will result in dismal hatching results.

You should move the eggs to the incubator as soon as possible after the last one is laid. If the eggs have not adhered to each other, bury each egg in the vermiculite so that one-third of it remains above the surface. Be careful to keep the eggs in the same position they were laid because turning them can damage or kill the embryo. If the eggs have already gotten stuck to each other, keep them together. Place them in the incubator with the bottom layer of eggs two-thirds buried. Whether you let the female incubate the eggs or you put them in an incubator, Chondro eggs will hatch in 39 to 65 days, the average time being around 50 days. In a given clutch, there can be hatchlings of any of the juvenile colors, but some clutches contain only hatchlings of one of the colors.

You can expect the same sorts of problems raising baby Chondros as when raising any of the other arboreal booids. Green Tree Python hatchlings cannibalize each other on occasion, so single housing is a must. Many keepers use a gallon jar with a screen lid, a perch, and a plant sprig growing hydroponically in a quarter-inch of water on the cage bottom as the cage fixtures. Others use moist paper towel as the substrate and forego the plant. If a water bowl is included or water covers the enclosure bottom, you must take precautions against the hatchlings drowning by having a plant or rock rising above the surface of the water. Hatchling Chondros should be kept at the same temperatures as the adults, with roughly 90% humidity. Like the young of the tree boas, hatchling Chondros are susceptible to respiratory infections if kept too dry.

Chondros are difficult feeders as hatchlings. The methods described earlier should help with all but the most stubborn of feeders. Baby Chondros are noted for insisting on geckos, skinks, and baby birds as first foods. Nearly all of these will switch to rodents eventually, but it may take quite a while. Several researchers note that Chondros that feed well turn green sooner than the ones that do not. Yellow young tend to turn green sooner than the red and brown ones. Fed well, these snakes will reach sexual maturity in about three years.

CONCLUSION

I hope this book helps you keep and breed these magnificent serpents. If you decide to go ahead on this great adventure, I urge you to read more, plan carefully, and keep the health and welfare of your animals at the forefront of you mind. Keeping and breeding the snakes in this book are still relatively new phenomena. As such, everyone working with these species should keep records and share what they find. There is plenty of room for everyone to contribute to the hobby.

A gorgeous yellow young Green Tree Python is a true sight to behold. Notice that the many small white spots, usually outlined with brown, tend to merge into larger spots and lines that may be retained by adults.

K. H. SWITAK

INDEX
Page numbers in **bold** indicate photographs